# Christmas for HARMONICA

## Easy solo arrangements with optional guitar and keyboard parts

JOSEPH STOEBENAU

Special thanks to Kyleen Denney,
Link Harnsberger, Bruce Goldes,
Steve Manus and Ron Manus.

Cover art: Steve Curtis

Alfred

MW00535155

# Christmas for HARMONICA

## Table of Contents

# How to Use This Book

This book was written for the harmonica to play the melody line of the songs. It is notated for C-diatonic harmonica, chromatic harmonica, and cross-harp style played on a C-diatonic harmonica. Although the music of all cross-harp arrangements is written an octave higher than it sounds, the hole numbers are correct. The cross-harp arrangements are more difficult than the diatonic arrangements due to the bent notes, so take your time and work up to them.

All that is needed to play the diatonic and cross harp arrangements is a harmonica in the key of C. The chromatic arrangements will work with both twelve- and sixteen-hole instruments.

Note: For more in-depth study of the harmonica please refer to Alfred's *Teach Yourself to Play Harmonica* book.

The piano chords are notated lead-sheet style above the melody line, and the guitar chord diagrams are on the top of the page.

While this book was written for the harmonica as a solo melodic instrument, the melody could be sung by a vocalist or played by another C-instrument, such as a flute or violin. A bass line could also be played by following the root motion of the chords.

# Harmonica Tablature Explained

## Notation

The diatonic harmonica has holes that are numbered 1 through 10. Under each musical note will be a number corresponding to the same number hole on the harmonica. This system will enable you to play the songs in this book even if you do not read music.

On the harmonica, tones can be produced either by blowing out or drawing in air.
This is notated using arrows:

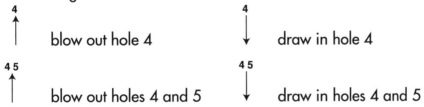

The length of an arrow indicates how long the note should sound.

If two or more notes are tied together, they will be notated as follows:

# *Cross-Harp Notation*

## Bent Notes

Bent notes can be achieved on the harmonica by drawing in and increasing the air pressure in the mouth cavity and dropping the jaw slightly. Although it is common to have a note sound as though it is being bent upwards, notes can only be bent downward on the harmonica. This is achieved by starting on the lowered tone (or bent note) and scooping upward into the desired note.

This is indicated by a bent arrow:    An angled arrow means to play only the "bent" or lowered part of a note:

A blow bend is notated with an upward curved arrow:  It is achieved by overblowing into a high numbered hole (usually 8, 9 and 10). When overblown, the tone will lower or bend downward.

## Chromatic Harmonica

There is only one symbol notated for the chromatic harmonica in this book: ⑤

A circle around a hole number means to push in the slide button to sound that note.

## Special Effects

A plus sign above a hole number ( $\overset{+}{4}$ ) means to cup your hands tightly around the harmonica.

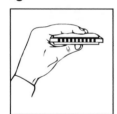 

This will produce a darker, muffled sound.

A circle above a hole number ( $\overset{o}{4}$ ) means to open the cupped part of your hands to produce a bright, open sound.

By combining the two, ( $\overset{+o}{4}$ ) a wah-wah effect can be achieved.

A wavy line ( ∿ ) means to add vibrato,

by moving the right hand open and closed around the harmonica:

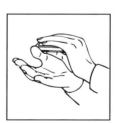

A sharp wavy line ( ⋀⋀ ) indicates a growl sound. This is produced by making a growl in your throat. This effect is easier to do on bent notes.

## Diatonic Harmonica

Because each diatonic harmonica is designed to play in a certain key, using a 10-hole diatonic harmonica in the key that it is designated is called playing straight harmonica. This book is written for a harmonica in the key of C.

Harmonicas in other keys will also work observing the tablature, although the accompanying instruments will have to adjust to match the harmonica key.

## Chromatic Harmonica

A chromatic harmonica allows a player to play all the notes in a chromatic scale by the use of a slide button. The most common chromatic harmonicas have 12 or 16 holes and cover a wider range than the diatonic harmonica.

## Cross Harp

Another term for cross harp is blues harp. A standard 10-hole diatonic harmonica is used, but now the draw 2 hole is the key center for the harmonica. A C harmonica played cross-harp style would play in the key of G. This book has special arrangements for cross harp. By playing cross-harp style, additional notes are obtained by bending notes on the draw holes.

# Angels We Have Heard On High

*Traditional*

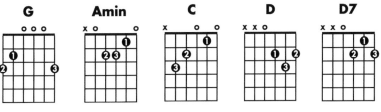

**G**   **Amin**   **C**   **D**   **D7**

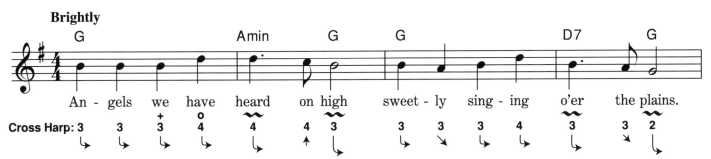

**Brightly**

An - gels we have heard on high sweet - ly sing - ing o'er the plains.

Cross Harp: 3  3  3  4  4  4  3  3  3  3  4  3  3  2

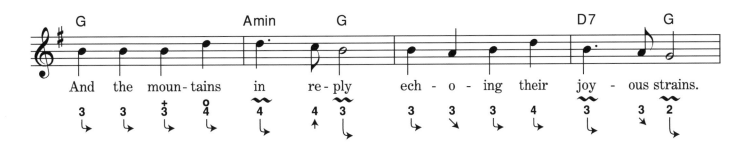

And the moun - tains in re - ply ech - o - ing their joy - ous strains.

3  3  3  4  4  4  3  3  3  3  4  3  3  2

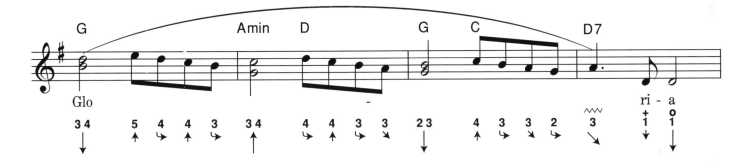

Glo - ri - a

3 4  5  4  4  3  3 4  4  4  3  3  2 3  4  3  3  2  3  1  1

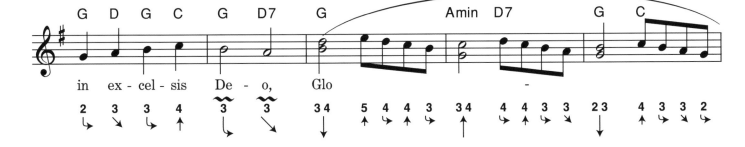

in ex - cel - sis De - o, Glo -

2  3  3  4  3  3  3 4  5  4  4  3  3 4  4  4  3  3  2 3  4  3  3  2

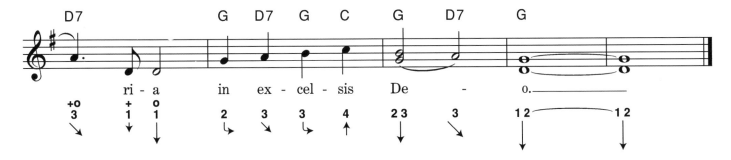

ri - a in ex - cel - sis De - o.

3  1  1  2  3  3  4  2 3  3  1 2  1 2

2. Shepherds, why this jubilee?
   Why your joyous strains prolong?
   What the gladsome tiding be
   Which inspire your heavenly song?

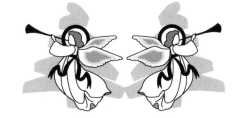

**Diatonic / Chromatic**

# Away In A Manger

Music by
James R. Murray

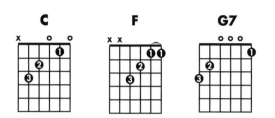

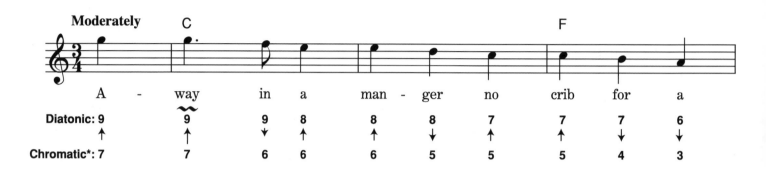

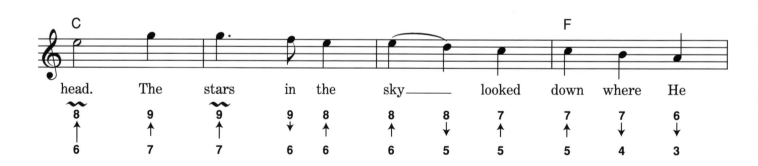

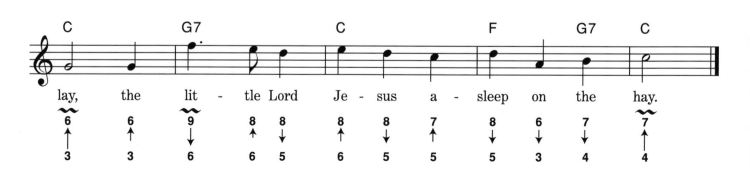

*Chromatic sounds an octave lower than written.

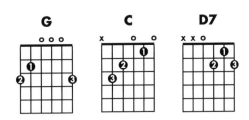

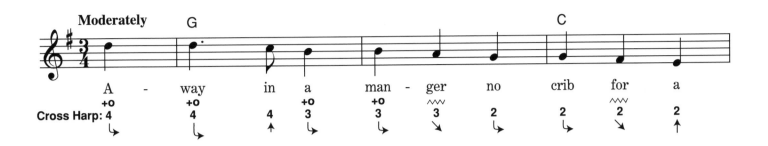

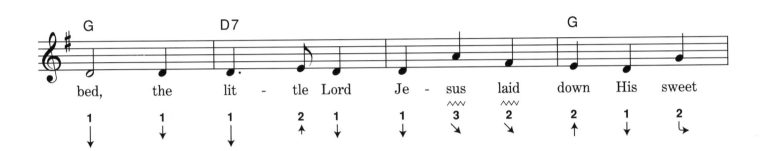

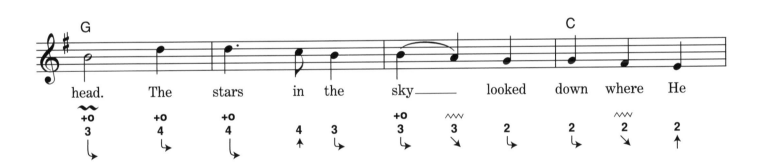

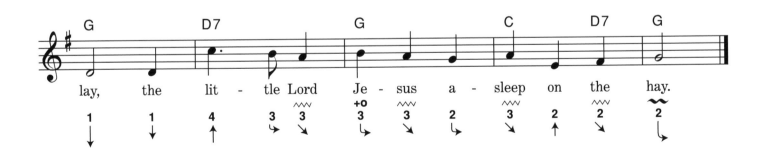

2. The cattle are lowing
   The baby awakes,
   But little Lord Jesus,
   No crying He makes.

I love Thee, Lord Jesus,
Look down from the sky,
And stay by my cradle
Till morning is nigh.

# Deck the Halls

*Old Welsh Air*

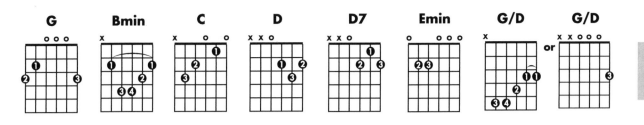

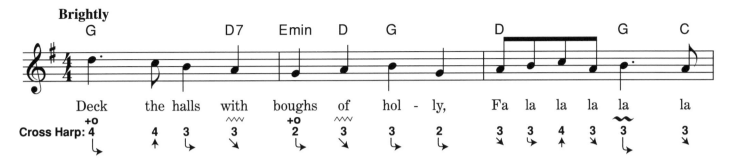

Deck the halls with boughs of hol - ly, Fa la la la la la

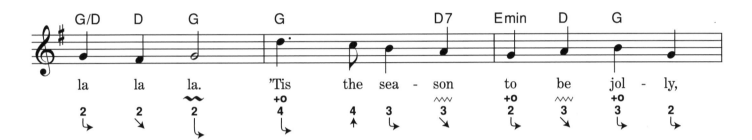

la la la. 'Tis the sea - son to be jol - ly,

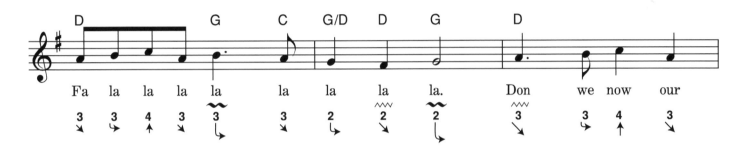

Fa la la la la la la la la. Don we now our

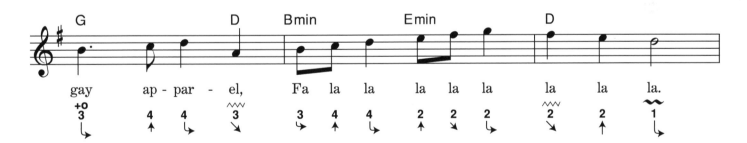

gay ap - par - el, Fa la la la la la la la la.

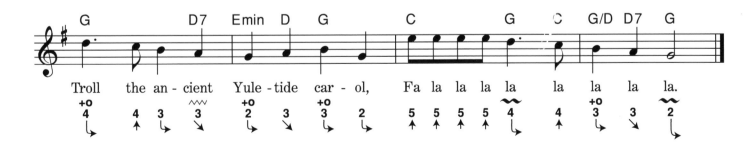

Troll the an - cient Yule - tide car - ol, Fa la la la la la la la la.

2. See the blazing Yule before us,  Follow me in merry measure,
   Fa la etc.  Fa la etc.
   Strike the harp and join the chorus,  While I tell of Yuletide treasure,
   Fa la etc.  Fa la etc.

**Diatonic / Chromatic**

# The First Noël

*Traditional*

# God Rest Ye Merry, Gentlemen

Diatonic / Chromatic

*Traditional*

*Chromatic sounds an octave lower than written.

# Good King Wenceslas

*Words by*
*Rev. John M. Neale*

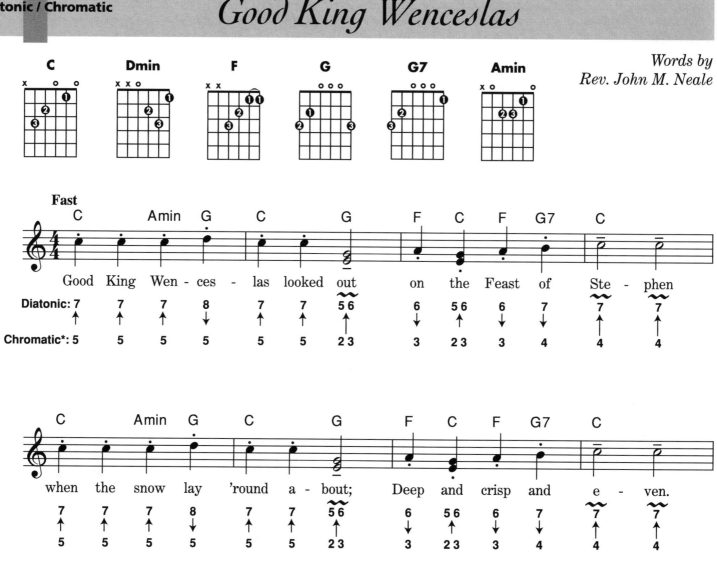

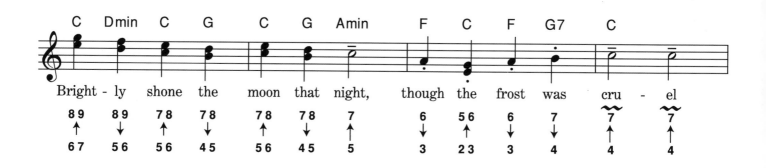

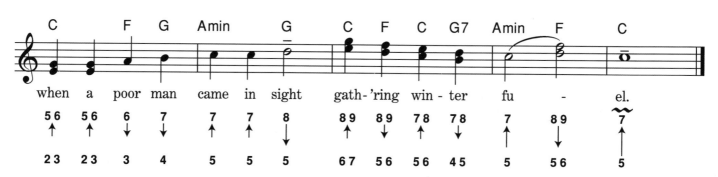

*Chromatic sounds an octave lower than written.

2. Hither page, and stand by me,
If thou know'st it telling
Yonder peasant, who is he?
Where and what his dwelling?
Sire, he lives a good league hence,
Underneath the mountain,
Right against the forest fence,
By St. Agnes's fountain.

3. Bring me flesh, and bring me wine,
Bring me pine logs hither;
Thou and I will see him dine,
When we bear them thither.
Page and monarch, forth they went,
Forth they went together,
Through the rude wind's wild lament,
And the bitter weather.

4. Sire, the night is darker now,
And the wind blows stronger,
Fails my heart, I know not how,
I can go no longer.
Mark my footsteps my good page,
Tread thou in them boldly.
Thou shalt find the winter's rage
Freeze thy blood less coldly.

5. In his master's steps he trod
Where the snow lay dinted,
Heat was in the very sod
Which the Saint had printed.
Therefore, Christian men, be sure,
Wealth or rank possessing,
Ye who now will bless the poor
Shall yourselves find blessing.

**Diatonic / Chromatic**

# Hark! The Herald Angels Sing

*Music by Felix Mendelssohn / Words by Charles Wesley*

# It Came Upon The Midnight Clear

**Diatonic / Chromatic**

*Words by*
*Rev. Edmund H. Sears*
*Music by*
*Richard S. Willis*

2. Still through the cloven skies they come
   With peaceful wings unfurled,
   And still their heavenly music floats
   O'er all the weary world;

   Above its sad and lowly plains
   They bend on hovering wing,
   And ever over its Babel sounds
   The blessed angels sing.

*Chromatic sounds an octave lower than written.

# Here We Come A-Wassailing

*Traditional English*

**Cross Harp**

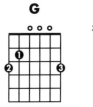 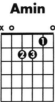     

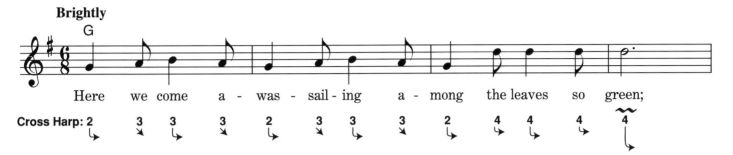

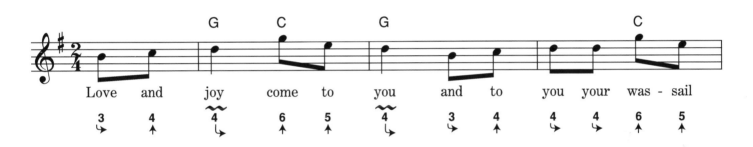

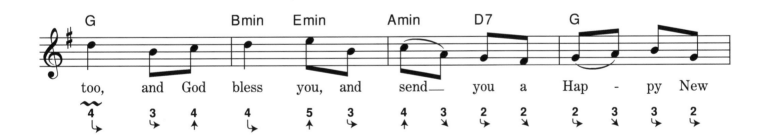

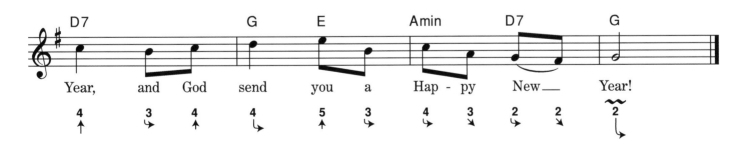

2. We are not daily beggars
That beg from door to door;
But we are neighbor children
Whom you have seen before:

3. We have got a little purse
Of stretching leather skin;
We want a little money
To line it well within:

4. God bless the master of this house,
Likewise the mistress too;
And all the little children
That round the table go:

# I Saw Three Ships

*Old English*

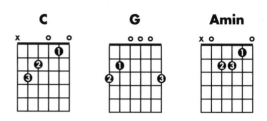

**C**   **G**   **Amin**

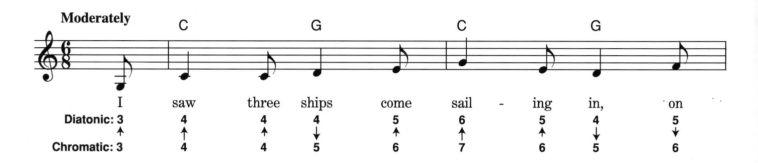

**Moderately**

C        G        C        G

I   saw   three   ships   come   sail  -  ing   in,   on

| Diatonic: | 3 | 4 | 4 | 4 | 5 | 6 | 5 | 4 | 5 |
| Chromatic: | 3 | 4 | 4 | 5 | 6 | 7 | 6 | 5 | 6 |

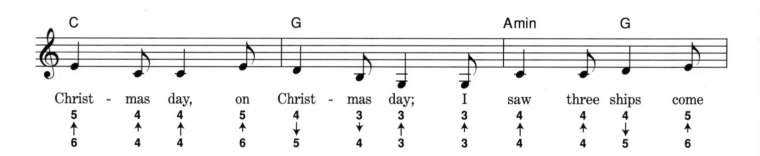

C                    G              Amin        G

Christ - mas   day,   on   Christ - mas   day;   I   saw   three   ships   come

| 5 | 4 | 4 | 5 | 4 | 3 | 3 | 3 | 4 | 4 | 4 | 5 |
| 6 | 4 | 4 | 6 | 5 | 4 | 3 | 3 | 4 | 4 | 5 | 6 |

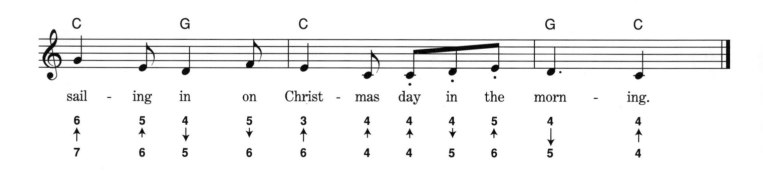

C        G        C                    G        C

sail - ing   in   on   Christ - mas   day   in   the   morn  -  ing.

| 6 | 5 | 4 | 5 | 3 | 4 | 4 | 4 | 5 | 4 | 4 |
| 7 | 6 | 5 | 6 | 6 | 4 | 4 | 5 | 6 | 5 | 4 |

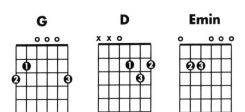

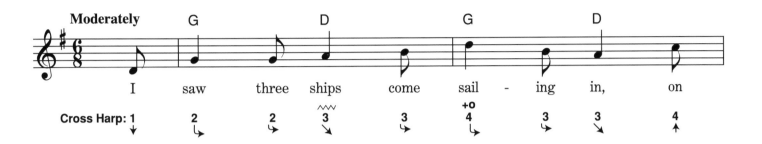

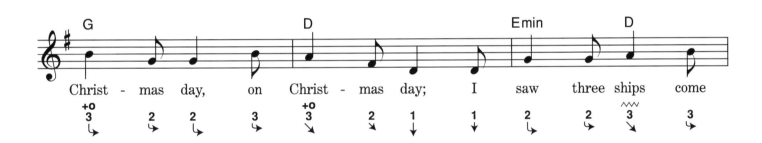

2. And what was in those ships all three,
   On Christmas Day, on Christmas Day;
   And what was in those ships all three,
   On Christmas Day, in the morning?

3. The Virgin Mary and Christ were there,
   On Christmas Day, on Christmas Day;
   The Virgin Mary and Christ were there,
   On Christmas Day in the morning.

**Diatonic / Chromatic**

# Jingle Bells

*J. Pierpont*

*Chromatic sounds an octave lower than written.

2. A day or two ago, I thought I'd take a ride;
   And soon Miss Fannie Bright was seated by my side.
   The horse was lean and lank, misfortune seemed his lot,
   He got into a drifted bank and we, got upsot!

3. Now the ground is white, go it while you're young;
   Take the girls tonight and sing this sleighing song.
   Just get a bobtail bay, two-forty for his speed,
   Then hitch him to an open sleigh and crack!
   You'll take the lead!

*Jingle Bells*
**Cross Harp**

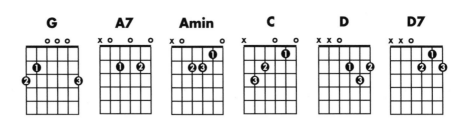

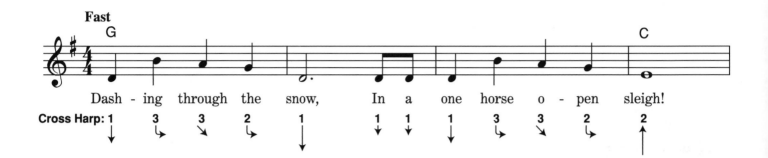

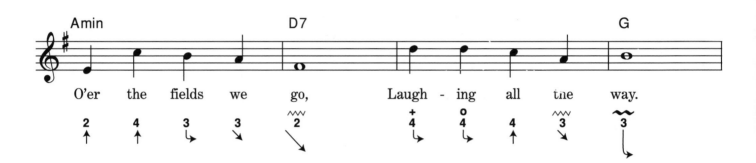

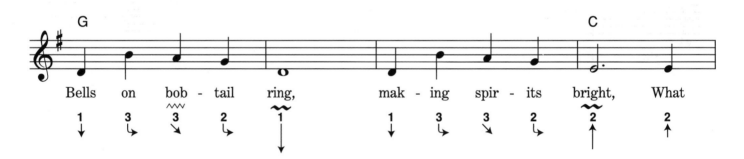

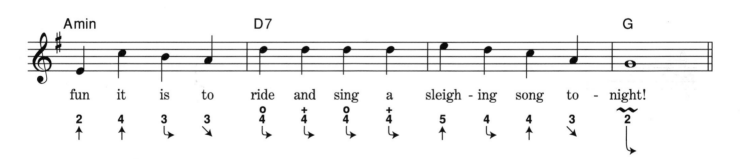

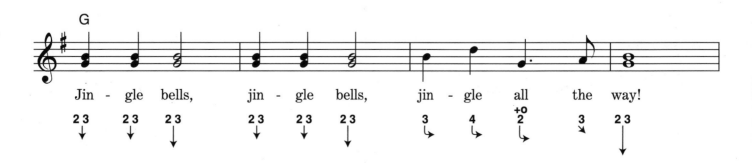

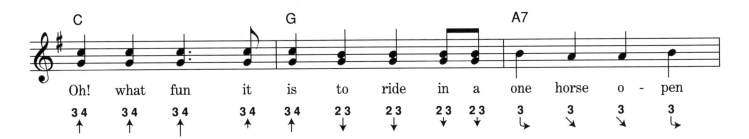

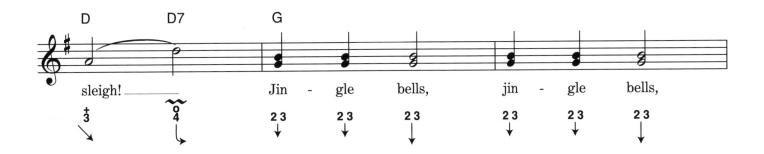

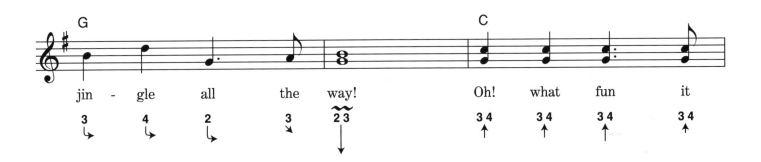

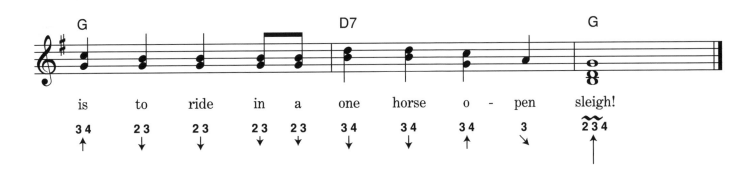

2. A day or two ago, I thought I'd take a ride;
   And soon Miss Fannie Bright was seated by my side.
   The horse was lean and lank, misfortune seemed his lot,
   He got into a drifted bank and we, got upsot!

3. Now the ground is white, go it while you're young;
   Take the girls tonight and sing this sleighing song.
   Just get a bobtail bay, two-forty for his speed,
   Then hitch him to an open sleigh and crack!
   You'll take the lead!

**Diatonic / Chromatic**

# Jolly Old St. Nicholas

*Traditional*

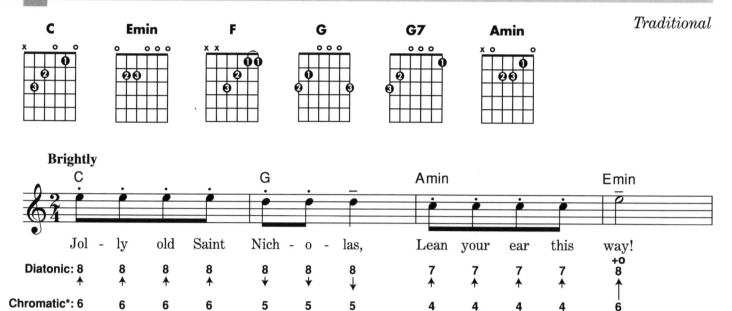

**Brightly**

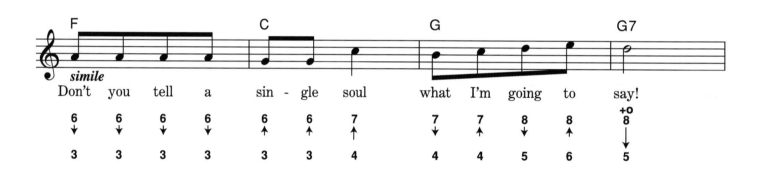

| | | | | | | | | | | | | |
|---|---|---|---|---|---|---|---|---|---|---|---|---|
| | Jol | ly | old | Saint | Nich | o | las, | Lean | your | ear | this | way! |
| **Diatonic:** | 8 | 8 | 8 | 8 | 8 | 8 | 8 | 7 | 7 | 7 | 7 | +o 8 |
| | ↑ | ↑ | ↑ | ↑ | ↓ | ↓ | ↓ | ↑ | ↑ | ↑ | ↑ | ↑ |
| **Chromatic\*:** | 6 | 6 | 6 | 6 | 5 | 5 | 5 | 4 | 4 | 4 | 4 | 6 |

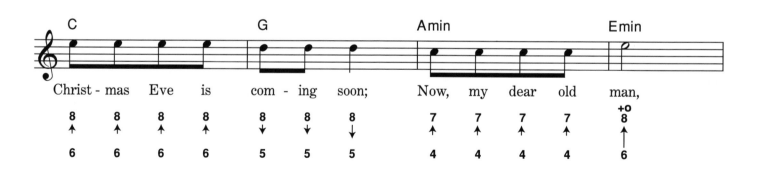

| | | | | | | | | | | | |
|---|---|---|---|---|---|---|---|---|---|---|---|
| Don't | you | tell | a | sin | gle | soul | what | I'm | going | to | say! |
| 6 | 6 | 6 | 6 | 6 | 6 | 7 | 7 | 7 | 8 | 8 | +o 8 |
| ↓ | ↓ | ↓ | ↓ | ↑ | ↑ | ↑ | ↓ | ↑ | ↓ | ↑ | ↓ |
| 3 | 3 | 3 | 3 | 3 | 3 | 4 | 4 | 4 | 5 | 6 | 5 |

*simile*

| | | | | | | | | | | | | |
|---|---|---|---|---|---|---|---|---|---|---|---|---|
| | Christ | mas | Eve | is | com | ing | soon; | Now, | my | dear | old | man, |
| | 8 | 8 | 8 | 8 | 8 | 8 | 8 | 7 | 7 | 7 | 7 | +o 8 |
| | ↑ | ↑ | ↑ | ↑ | ↓ | ↓ | ↓ | ↑ | ↑ | ↑ | ↑ | ↑ |
| | 6 | 6 | 6 | 6 | 5 | 5 | 5 | 4 | 4 | 4 | 4 | 6 |

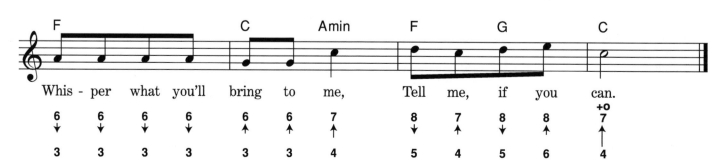

| | | | | | | | | | | | |
|---|---|---|---|---|---|---|---|---|---|---|---|
| Whis | per | what | you'll | bring | to | me, | Tell | me, | if | you | can. |
| 6 | 6 | 6 | 6 | 6 | 6 | 7 | 8 | 7 | 8 | 8 | +o 7 |
| ↓ | ↓ | ↓ | ↓ | ↑ | ↑ | ↑ | ↓ | ↑ | ↓ | ↑ | ↑ |
| 3 | 3 | 3 | 3 | 3 | 3 | 4 | 5 | 4 | 5 | 6 | 4 |

\*Chromatic sounds an octave lower than written.

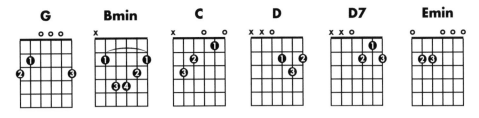

**Brightly**

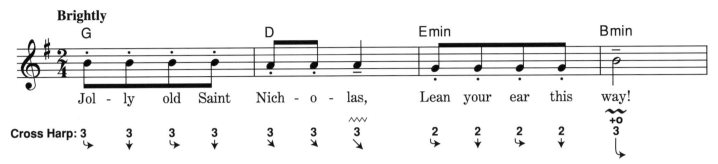

Jol - ly old Saint Nich - o - las, Lean your ear this way!

Cross Harp: 3 3 3 3 3 3 3 2 2 2 2 +o 3

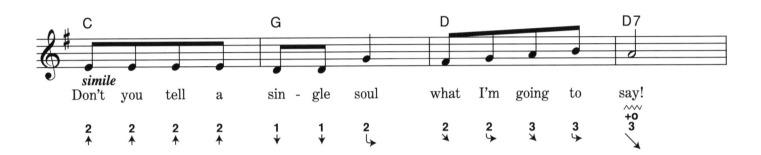

Don't you tell a sin - gle soul what I'm going to say!

*simile*

2 2 2 2 1 1 2 2 2 3 3 +o 3

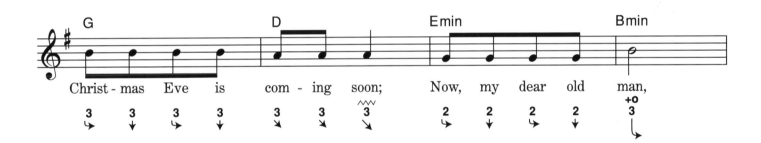

Christ - mas Eve is com - ing soon; Now, my dear old man,

3 3 3 3 3 3 3 2 2 2 2 +o 3

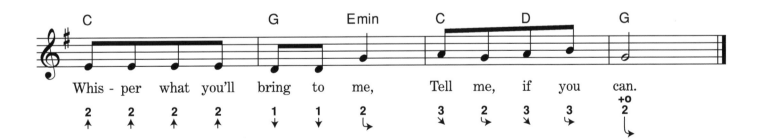

Whis - per what you'll bring to me, Tell me, if you can.

2 2 2 2 1 1 2 3 2 3 3 +o 2

2. When the clock is striking twelve,
When I'm fast asleep,
Down the chimney broad and black,
With your pack you'll creep.
All the stockings you will find
Hanging in a row;
Mine will be the shortest one,
You'll be sure to know.

3. Johnny wants a pair of skates,
Susy wants a sled;
Nellie wants a picture book
Yellow, blue and red;
Now I think I'll leave to you
What to give the rest;
Choose for me, dear Santa Claus,
You will know the best.

**Diatonic / Chromatic**

# Joy to the World

Words by
Issac Watts
Music by
G.F. Handel

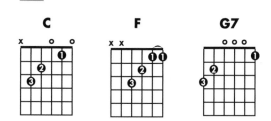

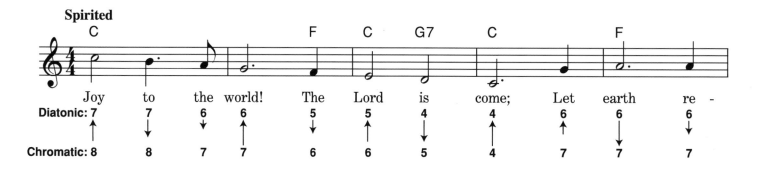

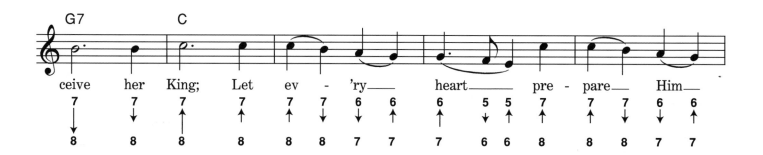

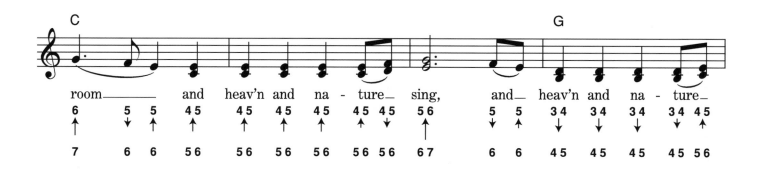

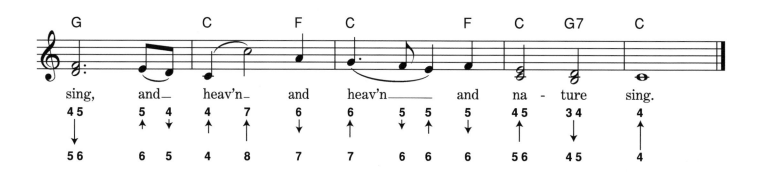

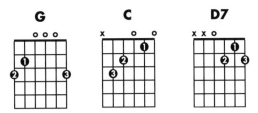

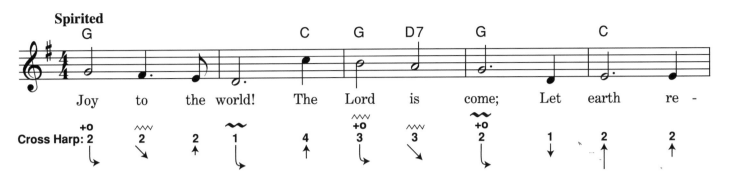

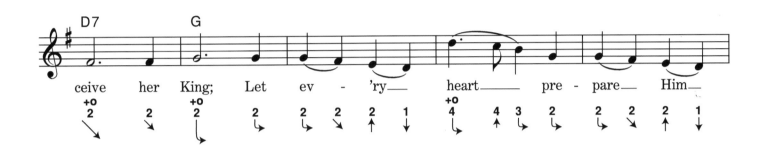

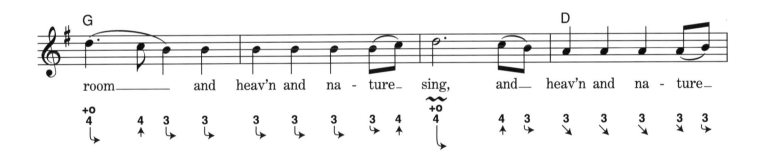

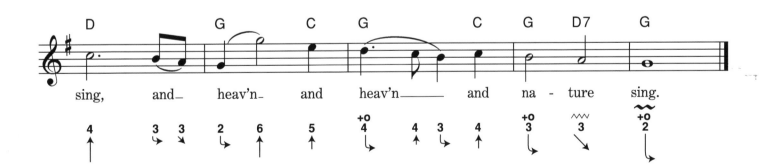

2. Joy to the World!  The Savior reigns;
   Let men their songs employ;
   While field and floods,
   Rocks, hills and plains,
   Repeat the sounding joy,
   Repeat the sounding joy,
   Repeat, repeat the sounding joy.

3. He rules the world!  With truth and grace;
   And makes the nations prove
   The glories of His righteousness,
   And wonders of His love,
   And wonders of His love,
   And wonders, wonders of His love.

**Diatonic / Chromatic**

# O Christmas Tree

*Old German Carol*

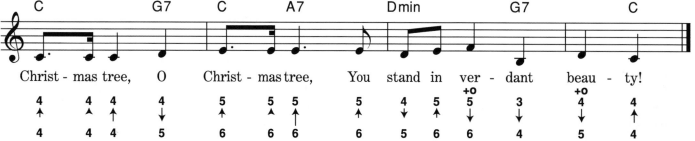

 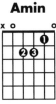  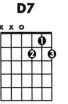 

G    Amin    C    D7    E7

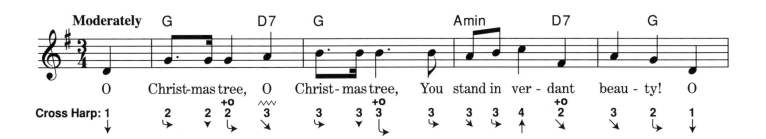

Moderately

O Christ-mas tree, O Christ-mas tree, You stand in ver-dant beau-ty! O

Cross Harp: 1   2   2   +o 2   3   3   3   +o 3   3   3   3   4   +o 2   3   2   1

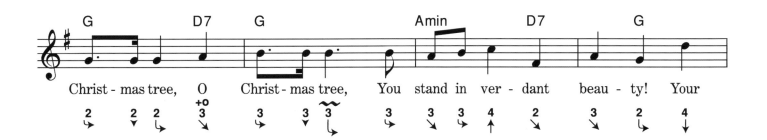

Christ-mas tree, O Christ-mas tree, You stand in ver-dant beau-ty! Your

2   2   2   +o 3   3   3   3   3   3   3   4   2   3   2   4

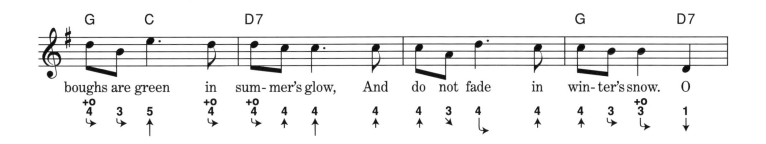

boughs are green in sum-mer's glow, And do not fade in win-ter's snow. O

+o 4   3   5   +o 4   +o 4   4   4   4   4   3   4   4   4   3   +o 3   1

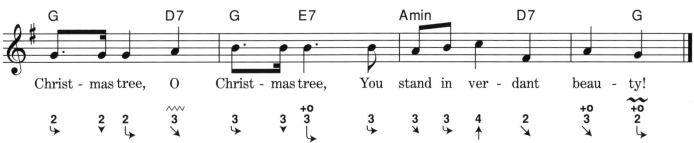

Christ-mas tree, O Christ-mas tree, You stand in ver-dant beau-ty!

2   2   2   3   3   3   +o 3   3   3   3   4   2   +o 3   +o 2

2. O Christmas Tree! O Christmas Tree,
   Much pleasure doth thou bring me!
   O Christmas Tree, O Christmas Tree,
   Much pleasure doth thou bring me!
   For ev'ry year the Christmas Tree,
   Brings to us all both joy and glee.
   O Christmas Tree! O Christmas Tree,
   Much pleasure doth thou bring me!

3. O Christmas Tree! O Christmas Tree!
   Thy candles shine out brightly!
   O Christmas Tree! O Christmas Tree,
   Thy candles shine out brightly!
   Each bough doth hold its tiny light,
   That makes each toy to sparkle bright,
   O Christmas Tree! O Christmas Tree,
   Thy candles shine out brightly!

Diatonic / Chromatic

# O Come, All Ye Faithful

Words by
*Frederick Oakeley*

Music by
*John F. Wade*

*Chromatic sounds an octave lower than written.

2. O sing, choirs of angels,
   Sing in exultation, O sing,
   All ye citizens of heaven above.
   Glory to God in the highest!

**Diatonic / Chromatic**

# *O Holy Night*

*Adolphe Adam*
*English words*
*by J.S. Dwight*

2. Truly He taught us to love one another,
His law is love, and His gospel is peace;
Chains shall He break for the slave is our brother,
And in His name all oppression shall cease.
Sweet hymns of joy in grateful chorus raise we,

Let all within us praise His holy name;
Christ is the Lord, oh, praise His name forever!
His pow'r and glory ever more proclaim!
His pow'r and glory ever more proclaim!

# O Holy Night
**Cross Harp**

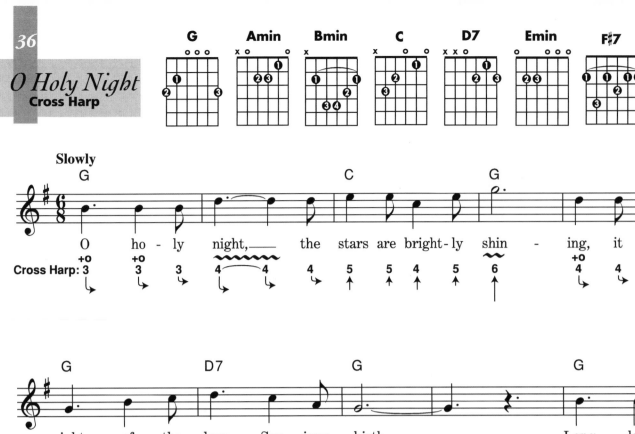

**Slowly**

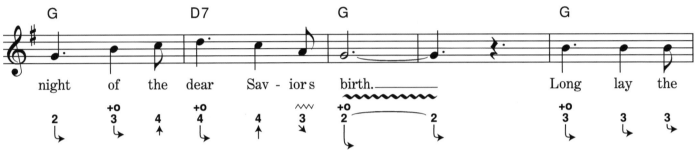

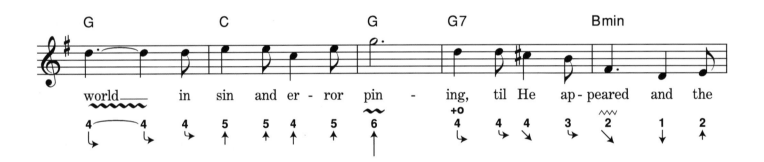

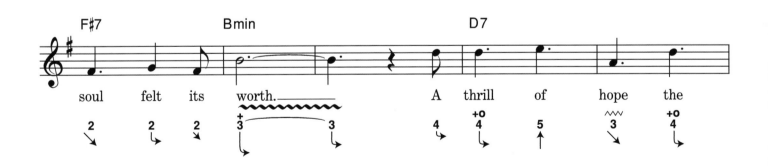

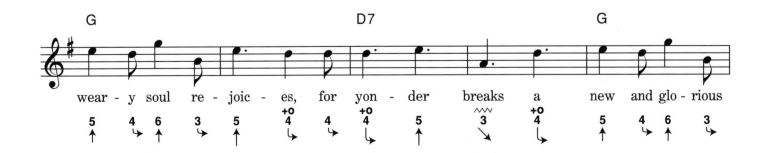

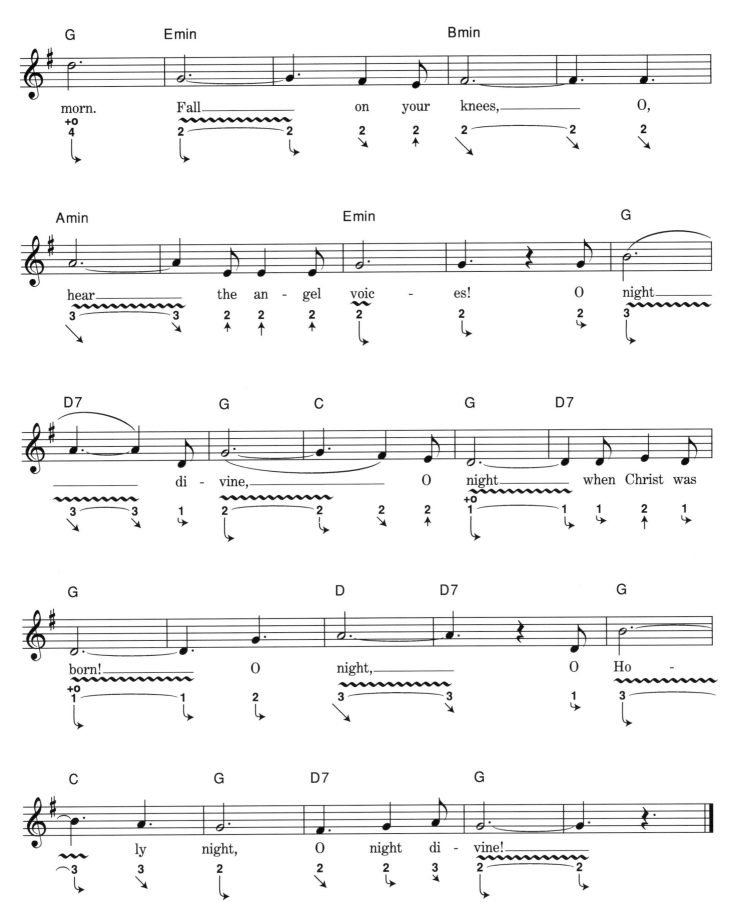

2. Truly He taught us to love one another,
His law is love, and His gospel is peace;
Chains shall He break for the slave is our brother,
And in His name all oppression shall cease.
Sweet hymns of joy in grateful chorus raise we,

Let all within us praise His holy name;
Christ is the Lord, oh, praise His name forever!
His pow'r and glory ever more proclaim!
His pow'r and glory ever more proclaim!

**Diatonic / Chromatic**

# O Little Town of Bethlehem

*Music by*
*Lewis H. Redner*
*Words by*
*Phillips Brooks*

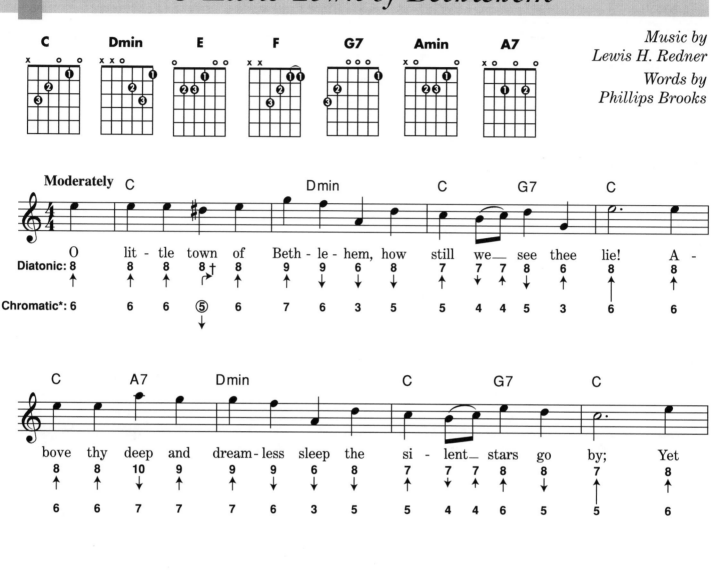

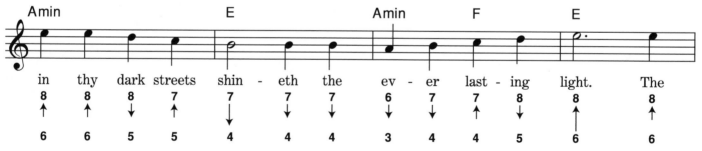

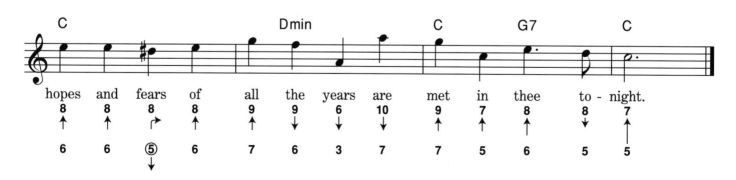

*Chromatic sounds an octave lower than written.
†Blow bend, see page 4, Cross Harp Notation.

# What Child Is This?

*Old English*

2. So bring Him incense, gold and myrrh,
   Come peasant king to own Him;
   The King of kings salvation brings,
   Let loving hearts enthrone Him.

   Raise, raise the song on high,
   The Virgin sings her lullaby;
   Joy, joy for Christ is born,
   The Babe, the Son of Mary.

*This arrangement sounds an octave lower than written.

**Diatonic / Chromatic**

# *Silent Night*

*Words by*
*Joseph Mohr*
*Music by*
*Franz Grüber*

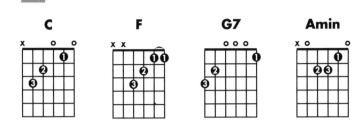

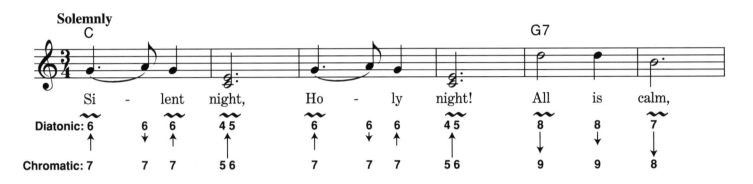

Si - lent night, Ho - ly night! All is calm,

| | | | | | | | | | |
|---|---|---|---|---|---|---|---|---|---|
| Diatonic: 6 | 6 | 6 | 4 5 | 6 | 6 | 6 | 4 5 | 8 | 8 | 7 |
| Chromatic: 7 | 7 | 7 | 5 6 | 7 | 7 | 7 | 5 6 | 9 | 9 | 8 |

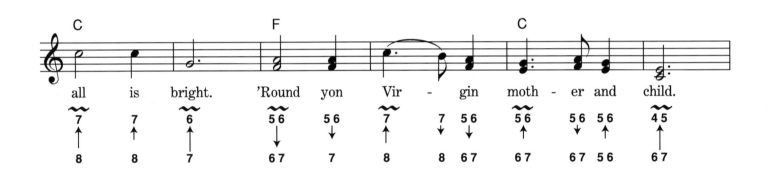

all is bright. 'Round yon Vir - gin moth - er and child.

| | | | | | | | | | |
|---|---|---|---|---|---|---|---|---|---|
| 7 | 7 | 6 | 5 6 | 5 6 | 7 | 7 | 5 6 | 5 6 | 5 6 | 5 6 | 4 5 |
| 8 | 8 | 7 | 6 7 | 7 | 8 | 8 | 6 7 | 6 7 | 6 7 | 5 6 | 6 7 |

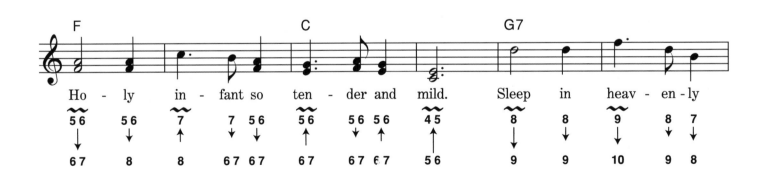

Ho - ly in - fant so ten - der and mild. Sleep in heav - en - ly

| | | | | | | | | | |
|---|---|---|---|---|---|---|---|---|---|
| 5 6 | 5 6 | 7 | 7 5 6 | 5 6 | 5 6 5 6 | 4 5 | 8 | 8 | 9 | 8 7 |
| 6 7 | 8 | 8 | 6 7 6 7 | 6 7 | 6 7 6 7 | 5 6 | 9 | 9 | 10 | 9 8 |

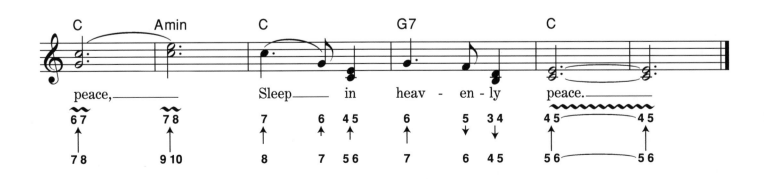

peace,_____ Sleep____ in heav - en - ly peace._____

| | | | | | | |
|---|---|---|---|---|---|---|
| 6 7 | 7 8 | 7 | 6 4 5 | 6 | 5 3 4 | 4 5 | 4 5 |
| 7 8 | 9 10 | 8 | 7 5 6 | 7 | 6 4 5 | 5 6 | 5 6 |

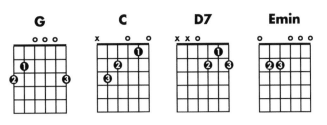

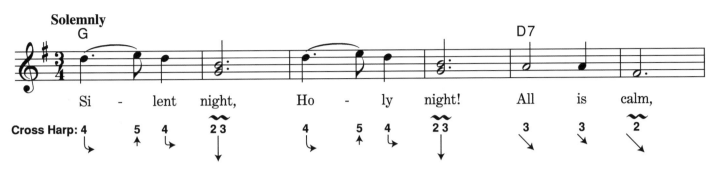

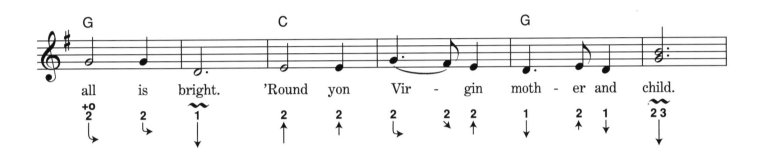

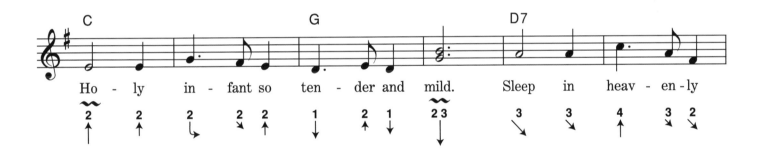

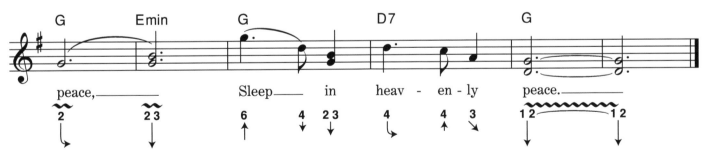

2. Silent night, holy night!
Shepherds quake at the sight.
Glories stream from heaven afar,
Heavenly hosts sing Alleluia,
Christ the Savior is born!
Christ the Savior is born.

3. Silent night, holy night!
Son of God, love's pure light.
Radiant beams from Thy holy face,
With the dawn of redeeming grace,
Jesus Lord at Thy birth.
Jesus Lord at Thy birth.

**Diatonic / Chromatic**

# Up On the Housetop

*Traditional*

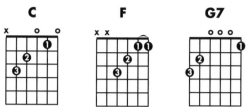

**Spirited**

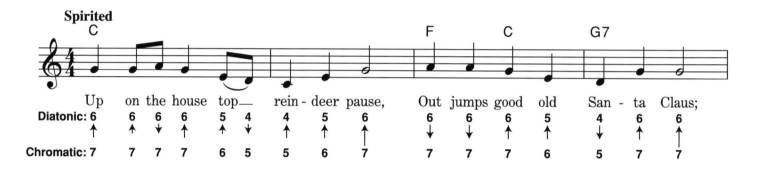

Up    on the house top— rein - deer pause,    Out  jumps good  old    San - ta  Claus;

| Diatonic: | 6 | 6 | 6 | 6 | 5 | 4 | 4 | 5 | 6 | 6 | 6 | 6 | 5 | 4 | 6 | 6 |
| Chromatic: | 7 | 7 | 7 | 7 | 6 | 5 | 5 | 6 | 7 | 7 | 7 | 7 | 6 | 5 | 7 | 7 |

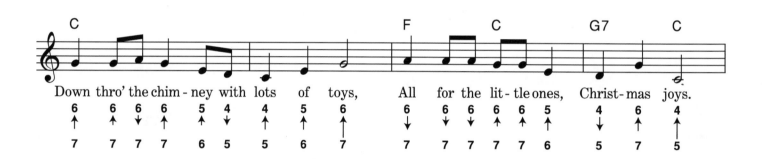

Down thro' the chim - ney with  lots   of  toys,    All   for the lit - tle ones,  Christ-mas  joys.

| 6 | 6 | 6 | 6 | 5 | 4 | 4 | 5 | 6 | 6 | 6 | 6 | 6 | 5 | 4 | 6 | 4 |
| 7 | 7 | 7 | 7 | 6 | 5 | 5 | 6 | 7 | 7 | 7 | 7 | 7 | 6 | 5 | 7 | 5 |

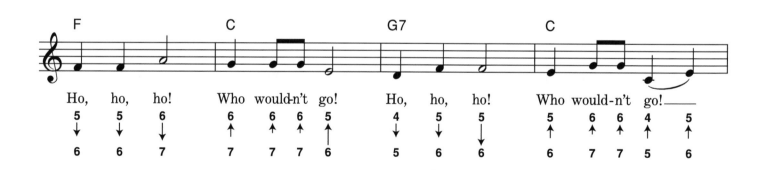

Ho,    ho,    ho!     Who would-n't go!    Ho,    ho,    ho!    Who would-n't    go!—

| 5 | 5 | 6 | 6 | 6 | 6 | 5 | 4 | 5 | 5 | 5 | 6 | 6 | 4 | 5 |
| 6 | 6 | 7 | 7 | 7 | 6 | 5 | 6 | 6 | 6 | 7 | 7 | 5 | 6 |

Up    on the house - top   click, click, click.  Down thro' the chim - ney with good Saint Nick.

| 6 | 6 | 6 | 6 | 5 | 5 | 6 | 6 | 6 | 6 | 6 | 6 | 5 | 5 | 4 | 6 | 4 |
| 7 | 7 | 7 | 7 | 6 | 6 | 7 | 7 | 7 | 7 | 7 | 7 | 6 | 6 | 5 | 7 | 5 |

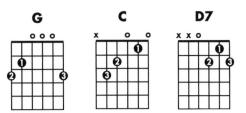

**Spirited**

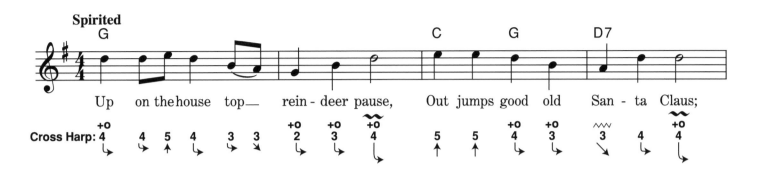

Up   on the house top— rein - deer pause,   Out jumps good old   San - ta Claus;

**Cross Harp:**

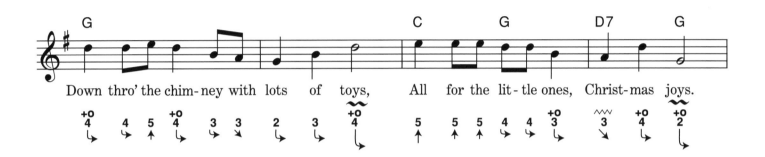

Down thro' the chim-ney with lots   of   toys,   All   for the lit - tle ones,  Christ-mas joys.

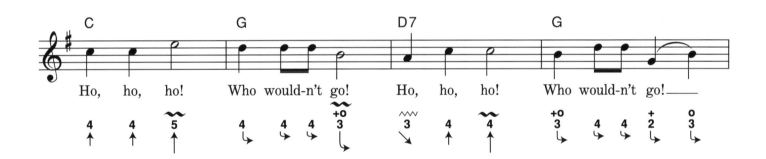

Ho,   ho,   ho!   Who would-n't go!   Ho,   ho,   ho!   Who would-n't go!___

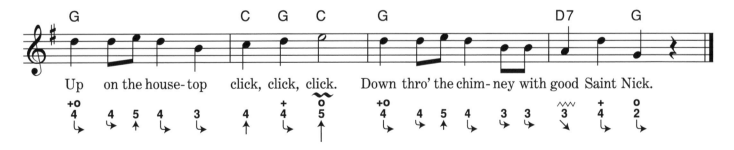

Up   on the house-top   click, click, click.   Down thro' the chim-ney with good Saint Nick.

2. First comes the stocking of little Nell;
   Oh, dear Santa, fill it well;
   Give her a dolly that laughs and cries,
   One that will open and shut her eyes.

**Diatonic / Chromatic**

# We Three Kings of Orient Are

*John H. Hopkins*

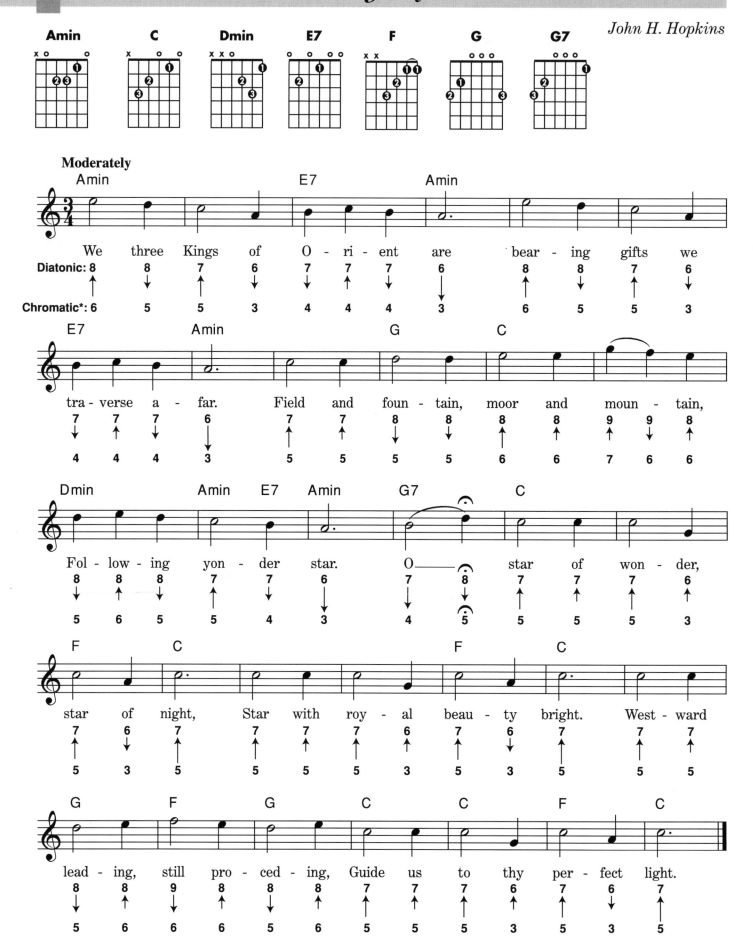

*Chromatic sounds an octave lower than written.

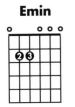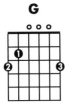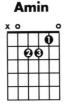

**Moderately**

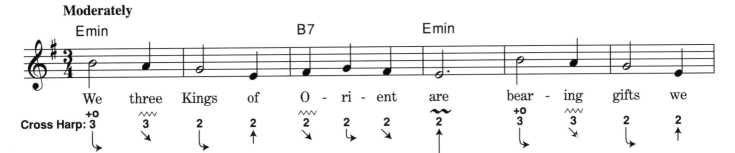

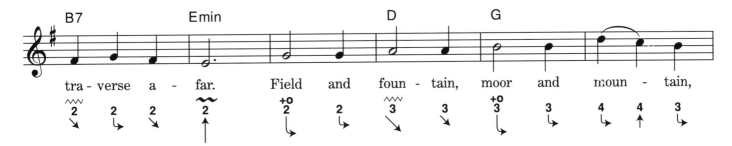

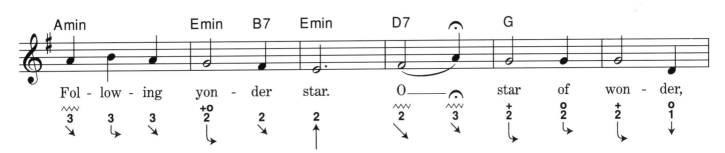

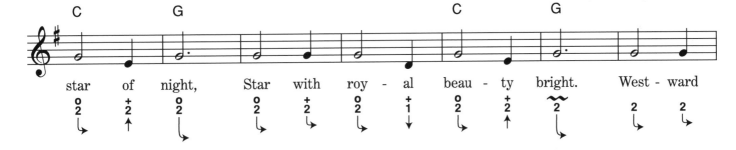

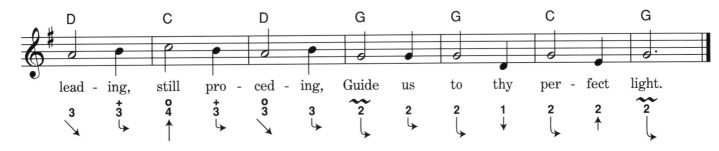

2. Born a king on Bethlehem's plain,
Gold I bring to crown Him again,
King forever, ceasing never
Over us all to reign.

3. Frankincense to offer have I;
Incense owns a Deity nigh;
Prayer and praising all men raising,
Worship Him, God on high.

4. Glorious now behold Him arise,
King and God and sacrifice;
Alleluia, Alleluia!
Sounds through the earth and skies.

**Diatonic / Chromatic** *We Wish You A Merry Christmas*

*Old English*

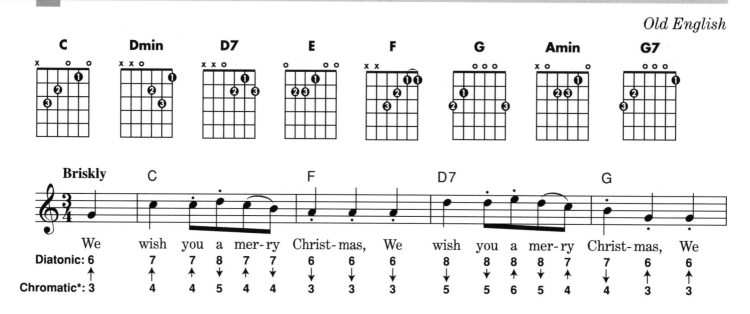

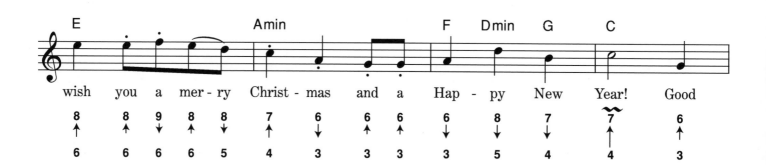

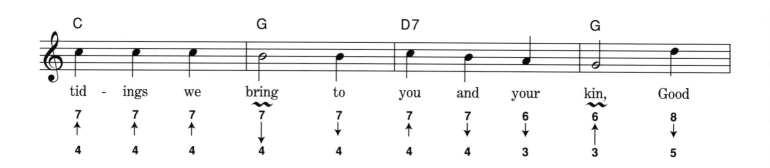

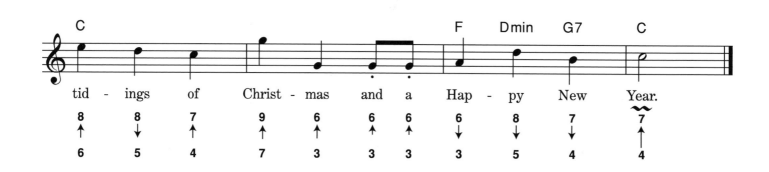

*Chromatic sounds an octave lower than written.

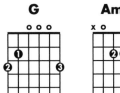 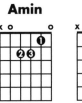  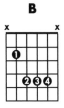 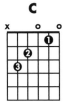 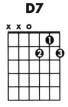  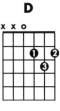

G  Amin  A7  B  C  D7  Em  D

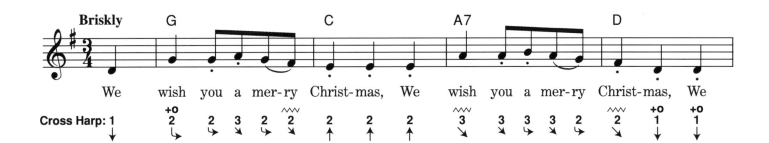

Briskly

G      C      A7      D

We wish you a mer-ry Christ-mas, We wish you a mer-ry Christ-mas, We

**Cross Harp:** 1

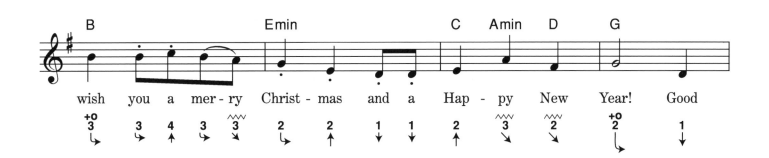

B      Emin      C Amin D G

wish you a mer-ry Christ - mas and a Hap - py New Year! Good

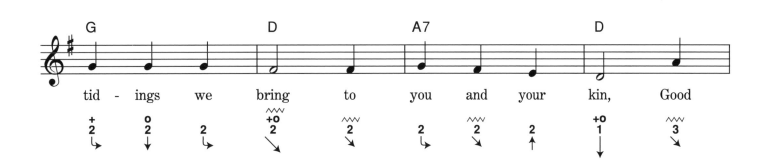

G      D      A7      D

tid - ings we bring to you and your kin, Good

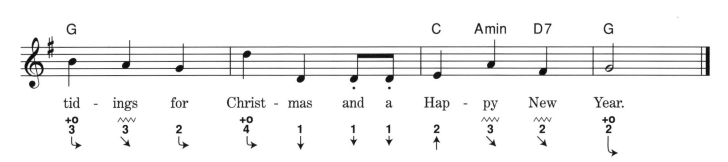

G      C Amin D7 G

tid - ings for Christ-mas and a Hap - py New Year.

# Master Chart of Notes on the Harmonica